The Way of the Cross
for Children

Kathryn Mulderink, OCDS

with drawings by
Father Victor KyNam

© Copyright by Kathryn Mulderink 2006, 2008
All rights reserved.

Other books by Kathryn Mulderink include:
Walk New: A Lenten Resource

Published by
Bezalel Books
Waterford, MI
www.BezalelBooks.com

Printed in the United States of America

No part of this book may be reproduced, stored in a retrieval system, or transmitted by any means, electronic, mechanical, photocopying, recording, or otherwise, without written permission from the author.

Cover design by Clare Mulderink

ISBN 978-0-9800483-7-7
Library of Congress Control Number 2008931071

Acknowledgements

For every finished project, there are many people who have contributed in ways that are easily overlooked, and I owe a debt of gratitude to many more than I can name. But I must at least say thank you to all who encouraged me to get these meditations into print; to Victor KyNam for his willingness to produce such beautiful and inspired drawings on short notice; to Linda Palmer for her proofreading and suggestions; to my daughter, Clare, for her work on the graphics; and to all my children, for whom I originally put this book together - they were the inspiration and "test subjects" for these Stations, having used them for several Lenten seasons.

I pray you find some good in them, and that God will bless your family as you recall His goodness and mercy.

February 11, 2006
Our Lady of Lourdes

by Samuel, age 4   *by Luke, age 6*

Write your own prayer to Jesus and draw your own picture on this page.

_____
_____
_____
_____
_____
_____
_____
_____
_____
_____
_____

Introductory Prayer

Jesus, I love You.
I want to walk with You as You carry the Cross
through the streets of Jerusalem, out of the city gates, and
up the hill where criminals are put to death.
As I walk with You, help me to understand
what You suffered to prove how much You love me
and to bring me to Heaven with You.

Mother Mary,
you walked along with Your Son, Jesus,
all the way to Calvary.
You know better than anyone how much He suffered
and how much He loves us.
And because of this, you love us too.
I want to walk along with you, praying next to you,
watching Jesus with you.
Help me to follow Him like you.

Amen.

First Station
Jesus is condemned to death

FIRST STATION
Jesus is condemned to death

We adore You, O Christ, and we bless You.
Because by Your holy Cross You have redeemed the world.

I THINK OF JESUS:
Jesus is standing before Pilate. Some soldiers are with Him.
His hands, which did so much good for people, are tied together.
On His head is a crown of sharp thorns and
He is bruised and bleeding all over because the soldiers
hit Him and scourged Him with whips.
Pilate says to the people,
"I am innocent of this blood; you crucify Him yourselves."
Pilate is thinking of himself and is afraid
of what the people will do if he goes against them.
Pilate does not want to face the truth.

I TALK TO JESUS:
Jesus, Pilate does not know that You are God,
but I know that You are.
You are the God Who made Pilate and made me.
You did not speak when the soldiers mocked You or spit on You.
You did not run away when Pilate said You must die.
You wanted to die for the Truth
so that I would be free to live with You forever.
Help me to always see what is true and do what is right,
even if others don't agree.
Teach me to love You as I should and help me to never sin again.

Jesus, You are so good to me;
You created me to always be.

SECOND STATION
JESUS TAKES HIS CROSS

SECOND STATION
Jesus takes His Cross

We adore You, O Christ, and we bless You.
Because by Your holy Cross You have redeemed the world.

I THINK OF JESUS:
Jesus is happy to see the big cross, because it is the key
that will open Heaven for us.
It is the way that He will use to show everyone that God is Love,
and Love will suffer even to death to save us from our sinfulness.
He does not complain or wish the cross was lighter;
He accepts it with hidden joy
to show us how to suffer and to love.

I TALK TO JESUS:
Jesus, You thought of me when You saw the cross.
You knew that by taking that cross,
I would be able to live with You forever in Heaven.
Help me to remember how much You love me
and to take up my cross every day and follow You, as You said.
Teach me how to say YES to everything You send me each day,
so that I will be more like You.
Teach me to love You as I should and help me never to sin again.

*Jesus, Brother, Lord, and Friend,
Help me say YES to all that You send.*

THIRD STATION
JESUS FALLS THE FIRST TIME

THIRD STATION
Jesus falls the first time

We adore You, O Christ, and we bless You.
Because by Your holy Cross You have redeemed the world.

I THINK OF JESUS:
Jesus is God, but He does not use His power
to make His cross easier.
He falls because the cross is so heavy and He is so weak
from the scourging and the rough treatment of the soldiers.
Our sins have made Him very, very sad.
But He wants us to be very, very happy, so He gets up and
continues to carry His cross all the way to the end.

I TALK TO JESUS:
Jesus, I want to help You carry Your cross.
You must have scraped Your knees on the stony ground and the
heavy cross hit Your bleeding head.
But You kept going, and kept giving.
I will be brave and keep going when things go wrong or I am hurt,
and I will be generous
in sharing all the things You have given me.
I will think of how much You suffered when You
stumbled and fell under the cross.
Teach me to love You as I should and help me never to sin again.

*When I am hurt or things go wrong,
Help me, Jesus, to be strong.*

FOURTH STATION
JESUS MEETS HIS MOTHER

FOURTH STATION
Jesus meets His Mother

We adore You, O Christ, and we bless You.
Because by Your holy Cross You have redeemed the world.

I THINK OF JESUS:
Jesus is sad that His Mother has to see Him
all covered with blood and dust and sweat.
Mary is so sad that her Son is being treated like a criminal and
dragged through the streets with no one to help Him.
He does not look like her little boy, Jesus,
and everyone is making fun of Him.
But she remembers that she told the angel:
"Be it done to me according to your word."
So she accepts this as the Father's will.

I TALK TO JESUS:
Jesus, I know You were happy to see Your Mother,
because You love her so much.
Mothers are never happy to see their children suffer, but
Mary knew You were doing Your Father's work;
she knew that You had to die so that I could live forever with You,
but it hurt her Heart to see You suffering so much.
Help me to love Mary as my Mother and be good to her.
Teach me to love you as I should and help me never to sin again.

*Jesus, You are my older brother,
And we both love the same holy Mother.*

FIFTH STATION
JESUS IS HELPED BY SIMON

FIFTH STATION
Jesus is helped by Simon

We adore You, O Christ, and we bless You.
Because by Your holy Cross You have redeemed the world.

I THINK OF JESUS:
Jesus could have had the angels carry His cross, but He did not.
The soldiers don't want Him to die before they crucify Him,
so they make Simon the Cyrenian help Him the rest of the way.
At first, Simon is afraid and wants to run away, but
You want to give him the gift of helping You.
And he helps You all the way to the end.
His sons, Rufus and Alexander, would help build the Church,
proud of what their father had done that day.

I TALK TO JESUS:
Jesus, I want to help You like Simon did,
and You want to give me the chance to help You.
I can help You by making little sacrifices and not complaining,
and by helping the people around me.
I will try to see You in all those who need help and
I will pray for everyone
so they will know how much You love them.
Teach me to love you as I should and help me never to sin again.

Jesus, though my heart is small,
Help me bring Your love to all.

SIXTH STATION
VERONICA WIPES THE FACE OF JESUS

SIXTH STATION
Veronica wipes the face of Jesus

We adore You, O Christ, and we bless You.
Because by Your holy Cross You have redeemed the world.

I THINK OF JESUS:
Jesus does not look like Himself;
His face is all covered with blood and bruised and swollen.
He cannot see well because of the blood in His eyes.
Veronica feels very sorry for Him and risks making the soldiers
angry by stepping out of the crowd and
wiping His face with her veil.
Jesus is grateful and leaves a picture of His face on her veil.

I TALK TO JESUS:
Jesus, I have more than Your picture on my soul.
You are really there, Jesus, with the Father and the Holy Spirit.
Just as our sins made Your beautiful face bruised and bloody,
help me to realize that sin makes it hard to see You in me.
But when I help others like Veronica did,
Your face shines through me to others.
Help me to be as brave as Veronica in doing good to others.
Teach me to love you as I should and help me never to sin again.

*Being kind to others makes Your Face clear
And helps them know that You are near.*

SEVENTH STATION
JESUS FALLS THE SECOND TIME

SEVENTH STATION
Jesus falls the second time

We adore You, O Christ, and we bless You.
Because by Your holy Cross You have redeemed the world.

I THINK OF JESUS:
Jesus is very tired from carrying the heavy cross
and he falls again.
He falls to the ground and scrapes His knees and His hands.
The soldiers hit Him and yell at Him to get up.
He is thinking of us as He struggles to get back on His feet.
He knows that He must keep going to the end
so that He can cancel our sins and make us friends of God.

I TALK TO JESUS:
Jesus, it hurts You all over to fall again.
Your body is weak and Your head hurts so much.
My sins made You fall under the cross,
but Your love for me made You get back up again.
You were teaching us that every time we are weak and fall,
we should ask You for the strength to try again to be good.
Teach me to love You as I should and help me never to sin again.

Lord Jesus, I see You sad and alone;
Please help to make my heart Your throne.

EIGHTH STATION
JESUS TALKS TO THE HOLY WOMEN

EIGHTH STATION
Jesus talks to the Holy Women

We adore You, O Christ, and we bless You.
Because by Your holy Cross You have redeemed the world.

I THINK OF JESUS:
Jesus sees some women who are crying for Him.
Even though He is very weak, He stops to gently tell them
to weep for their sins and the sins of the people around them,
because it is sin that makes Him suffer,
and it makes us unhappy too.

I TALK TO JESUS:
Jesus, I should cry for my sins too,
because they hurt You and others.
Every time I go to Confession, You forgive my sins
and talk to me through Your priest.
Thank You for this gift of mercy, which lets us
keep starting over again,
and gives us the grace we need to be good.
Teach me to love You as I should and help me never to sin again.

Lord Jesus, I want to start again for You;
Wash me clean and make me new.

NINTH STATION
JESUS FALLS THE THIRD TIME

NINTH STATION
Jesus falls the third time

We adore You, O Christ, and we bless You.
Because by Your holy Cross You have redeemed the world.

I THINK OF JESUS:
Jesus falls again to the ground, into the dust.
The soldiers cruelly pull to get Him up again to keep walking.
They don't care how weak He is;
they just keep yelling and hitting.
He gets back on His feet to show us how to keep going.

I TALK TO JESUS:
Jesus, help me to keep trying to be good,
even though sometimes I commit the same sins
over and over again.
I will try to think of You getting back up from the dust
and ask You to help me start over again every day.
If I am sorry, You will forgive me again and again, and
if I keep trying, You will give me the grace to be good.
Teach me to love You as I should and help me never to sin again.

Jesus, help me to be very good
And keep on trying as I should.

TENTH STATION
JESUS IS STRIPPED OF HIS CLOTHES

TENTH STATION
Jesus is stripped of His clothes

We adore You, O Christ, and we bless You.
Because by Your holy Cross You have redeemed the world.

I THINK OF JESUS:
Jesus has nothing now, not even His clothes.
The soldiers tear them off cruelly,
making all his wounds hurt and bleed again.
Jesus gives everything willingly,
even as the soldiers make fun of Him.
He shivers from the cold wind up on the hill,
and every part of Him is bleeding and hurting, but
He is still full of love for everyone.

I TALK TO JESUS:
Jesus, the soldiers hurt You over and over again.
When I am mean to others, I hurt You too,
because You live in their souls just as You do in mine.
I hurt You also when I am selfish,
because You gave everything for us,
even Your clothes and every drop of Your blood.
Help me to be kind and generous to others.
Teach me to give to others and not to take from them.
Teach me to love You as I should and help me never to sin again.

Lord Jesus, help me always to give and share;
This is how people will know that I care.

ELEVENTH STATION
JESUS IS NAILED TO THE CROSS

ELEVENTH STATION
Jesus is nailed to the Cross

We adore You, O Christ, and we bless You.
Because by Your holy Cross You have redeemed the world.

I THINK OF JESUS:
Jesus is laid on the Cross of cold, hard wood.
He opens His arms wide and does not fight the soldiers as they
hammer the nails into His hands and feet.
Jesus is doing what His Father wants, and
because He loves us so much, He accepts every bit of pain
to make us children of God.

I TALK TO JESUS:
Jesus, You only did good things with Your hands;
You healed the sick, embraced sinners, and broke bread for others.
Your feet carried You from town to town to reach others.
Now I am sad to see Your hands and feet wounded and bleeding,
nailed to the wood of the Cross.
Teach me to do only good things with my hands,
and to accept everything without complaining for love of You.
Teach me to love You as I should and help me never to sin again.

*Teach me to accept all things for love of You,
no matter what others say or do.*

TWELFTH STATION
JESUS DIES ON THE CROSS

TWELFTH STATION
Jesus dies on the Cross

We adore You, O Christ, and we bless You.
Because by Your holy Cross You have redeemed the world.

I THINK OF JESUS:
Jesus hangs on the Cross, with two criminals next to Him,
for three long hours. Some people are still making fun of Him,
but His Mother is there, and St. John, and Mary Magdalen.
Even while He was dying, He was thinking of others -
He forgave all those who hurt Him, and He
forgave the criminal who admitted he was wrong.
He gave us His perfect Mother to be our own.
Then He offered His soul to the Eternal Father.

I TALK TO JESUS:
Jesus, You love me and died for me.
I am very sorry that I have hurt You by sinning,
because You have proven that You love me so much.
You gave me everything, and even gave
Your whole self on the Cross.
Help me to realize how valuable my soul is,
that You were willing to suffer and die
so that I could live forever with You.
Teach me to love You as I should and help me never to sin again.

*Jesus, when I look at the Cross, I can see
that You gave everything for me.*

THIRTEENTH STATION
JESUS IS TAKEN DOWN FROM THE CROSS

THIRTEENTH STATION
Jesus is taken down from the Cross

We adore You, O Christ, and we bless You.
Because by Your holy Cross You have redeemed the world.

I THINK OF JESUS:
Jesus has opened Heaven with the new key, the Cross.
The soldier has made sure He is dead
by piercing His Heart with a spear,
so that the last drops of blood and water can be poured out.
Jesus has given everything for me.
Now His friends take Him down and
lay Him in His Mother's arms.
She is very sad, but she knows why He has died,
so she takes the whole world into Her Heart.
Now she is everyone's Mother.

I TALK TO JESUS:
Jesus, thank You for dying on the Cross for me.
You were obeying Your Father in Heaven
when You suffered for me.
To show You how much I love You,
I will obey my mother and father too.
Even after You were dead, You had more to give:
Your Heart was pierced
and You gave the last drops of Your blood.
Help me to always give to others, to find ways to help them,
and to think of others before myself.
Teach me to love You as I should and help me never to sin again.

Jesus, I will never go astray
Or make a mistake if I obey.

FOURTEENTH STATION
JESUS IS LAID IN THE TOMB

FOURTEENTH STATION
Jesus is laid in the tomb

We adore You, O Christ, and we bless You.
Because by Your holy Cross You have redeemed the world.

I THINK OF JESUS:
Jesus' lifeless body is wrapped in a sheet and
laid in a borrowed tomb.
A large stone is rolled in front of the opening.
His long, hard trip to Calvary is finished now.
He is silent.
His friends are very sad,
because they do not know that He will rise again.
They look on His closed eyes and do not understand
that they will soon see them opened again.
Then they will know that
Love is stronger than death.

I TALK TO JESUS:
Jesus, Your body is dead now, but death is never the end.
You are living forever, so every person will live forever.
Only our bodies enter the tomb; our souls are always alive in You.
Help me to keep my heart open to You always,
and to remember that You are my best Friend, alive forever.
Teach me to love You as I should and help me never to sin again.

Lord Jesus, death is not the end;
It is the moment when we see our Friend.

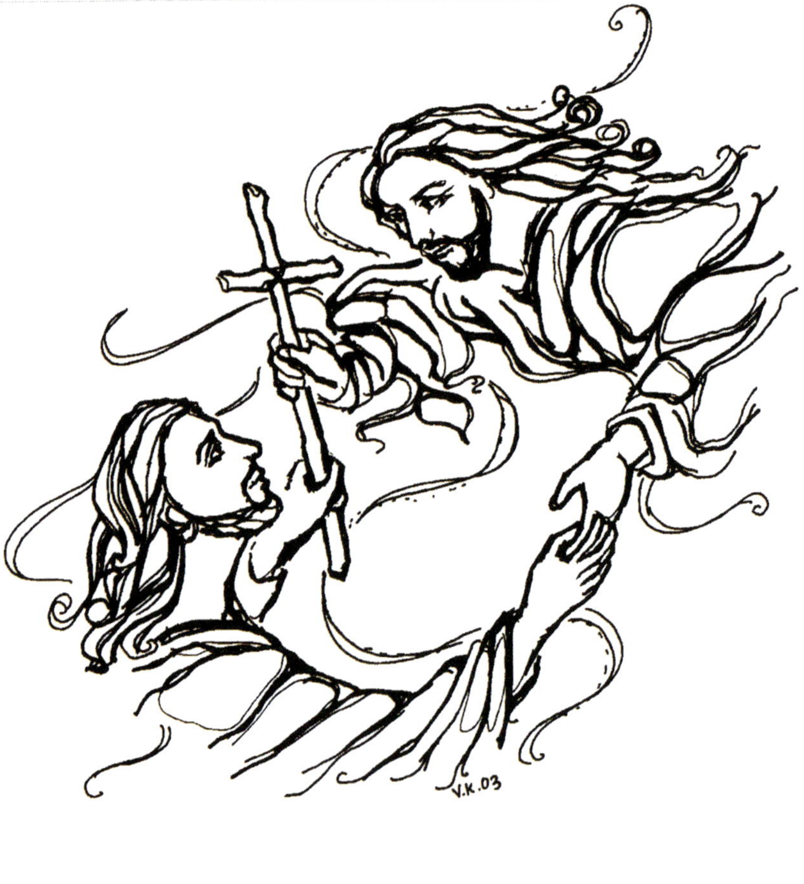
V.K.03

Closing Prayer

Jesus, on Easter morning, Your body will rise from the tomb and
You will continue to give and teach for forty more days.
Then You will go to Your Father in Heaven and
send the Holy Spirit to begin Your Church here on earth.
Even after You gave Your life for us, You had more to give.
And You continue to give us everything.

Help me to remember that You made me to love You,
that You died on the Cross and rose from the dead so that
I could be happy with You forever,
and that You are always helping me.
You are always with me.
And You love me no matter what.
I love You, Jesus.
Thank You for dying on the Cross for me.

Help me to remember that after every sadness, there is joy.
After every darkness, there is light.
After the sadness of Good Friday comes the joy of Easter,
and now You live and reign, with the Father and the Holy Spirit,
forever and ever.

Amen.

by Emma, age 8

by Rachel, age 8

Find a Scripture verse about Jesus that is special to you and write it here. Then draw a picture for it.

_____

_____

_____

_____

_____

Write a prayer or poem for Jesus to thank Him. Then decorate the page.

LaVergne, TN USA
15 October 2009
160972LV00001B